Afanasii Ivanovich Bulgakov, William John Birkbeck

The Question of Anglican Orders

Afanasii Ivanovich Bulgakov, William John Birkbeck

The Question of Anglican Orders

ISBN/EAN: 9783744773324

Printed in Europe, USA, Canada, Australia, Japan

Cover: Foto ©Suzi / pixelio.de

More available books at **www.hansebooks.com**

The Church Historical Society.

President :—THE RIGHT REVEREND M. CREIGHTON, D.D.,
LORD BISHOP OF LONDON.

Chairman :—THE REVEREND W. E. COLLINS,
PROFESSOR OF ECCLESIASTICAL HISTORY
AT KING'S COLLEGE, LONDON.

LV.

The Question of Anglican Orders

*In respect to a "Vindication" of the Papal decision, which was
drawn up by the English Roman Catholic Bishops
at the end of 1897.*

BY

A. BULGAKOFF,

PROFESSOR OF ECCLESIASTICAL HISTORY IN THE ECCLESIASTICAL
ACADEMY AT KIEFF.

TRANSLATED BY

W. J. BIRKBECK, M.A., F.S.A.

PUBLISHED UNDER THE DIRECTION OF THE TRACT COMMITTEE.

LONDON:
SOCIETY FOR PROMOTING CHRISTIAN KNOWLEDGE.
NORTHUMBERLAND AVENUE, W.C.; 43, QUEEN VICTORIA STREET, E.C.
BRIGHTON: 129, NORTH STREET.
NEW YORK: E. & J. B. YOUNG & CO.
1899.

The Church Historical Society.

President:—The Right Reverend M. Creighton, D.D.,
Lord Bishop of London.

Chairman:—The Reverend W. E. Collins,
Professor of Ecclesiastical History
at King's College, London.

LV.

The Question of Anglican Orders

In respect to a "Vindication" of the Papal decision, which was drawn up by the English Roman Catholic Bishops at the end of 1897.

BY

A. BULGAKOFF,

PROFESSOR OF ECCLESIASTICAL HISTORY IN THE ECCLESIASTICAL
ACADEMY AT KIEFF.

TRANSLATED BY

W. J. BIRKBECK, M.A., F.S.A.

PUBLISHED UNDER THE DIRECTION OF THE TRACT COMMITTEE.

LONDON:
SOCIETY FOR PROMOTING CHRISTIAN KNOWLEDGE.
Northumberland Avenue, W.C.; 43, Queen Victoria Street, E.C.
BRIGHTON: 129, North Street.
New York: E. & J. B. YOUNG & CO.
1899.

PREFACE.

—◦—

THE following article, by the eminent Russian scholar A. Bulgakoff, Professor of Ecclesiastical History in the Ecclesiastical Academy of Kieff, appeared in the "Transactions of the Kieff Ecclesiastical Academy" for August 1898, and is here translated for the benefit of English readers. It has been divided into sections for purposes of clearness, and a few explanatory notes by the translator and the present writer have their respective initials appended to them; otherwise, it appears exactly as it was written.

Its value at the present time, for Western readers, is very great; first, as illustrating the teaching of the Russian Church as to the theological value of the Orders of other bodies, and secondly, as giving a clear and acute criticism of the recent controversy on Anglican Orders, with the verdict of the writer in favour of the validity of those Orders, so far as historical and canonical criteria are concerned.

(1) It will be observed (p. 45) that the writer holds, in accordance with the teaching of the Church of which he is a member, that it is possible for the grace of the priesthood to be "extinguished" through heresy or schism even where the Apostolical Succession of Order has been preserved; and that strictly speaking this might be said to apply (not to any one body but) "to all non-Orthodox confessions." Consequently, in dealing with the matters in which the English Church is considered to be defective, he mentions amongst other things both "the doctrine of the *Filioque*"

A 2

and also "not only . . . its Protestant errors, but also . . . those many mediaeval novelties which have separated the English people from their Mother the primitive Catholic Church of the first nine centuries of her history" (p. 40). Professor Bulgakoff however does not attempt to give a decision as to whether the grace of the priesthood has been extinguished in the English Church ; since the "severe judgement" above alluded to has sometimes been softened by the Church on account of particular circumstances, and since in any case "the final decision of the question rests with the Church, and not with her individual representatives" (p. 45).

(2) This being so, the author's conclusions upon the historical and canonical questions involved may be received with the greater attention since he is in a position to enter upon the consideration of the matter without any bias for or against our Orders. It is therefore the more satisfactory to find that his conclusions on historical and canonical grounds are entirely favourable to us. In particular, attention must be called to what our author has to say with regard to the argument of the *Vindication of the Bull Apostolicae Curae.* He points out that, *pace* Cardinal Vaughan and his colleagues, "the validity of Orders does not depend upon the validity of the Sacrament of the Eucharist ; but on the contrary, upon the validity of the grace living in the minister, and given him by means of the laying on of the hands of the presbytery (1 Tim. iv. 14), depends the possibility of affording valid, and not merely sham, Sacraments" (p. 39).

To the English Churchman, of course, the matter does not present itself in precisely the same way as it does to the Russian scholar. Without in any way claiming to be exempt from human incompleteness and human error, we have ever held the Catholic Faith in its fullness as we received it from our fathers. Whilst recognizing that there have been many faults on our part in the past and in the present, we are yet well aware that we have never departed from the unity of the Catholic Church. We therefore confidently believe that the grace of our Orders remains unimpaired, as we are persuaded that historically and canonically alike our Succession is unassailable ; and we look forward to the time when both these things will be recognized throughout the whole Church. Meanwhile, we have no desire to hold back any of the facts. We willingly recognize the view which is held in a sister Church on the former point, and we cordially welcome this testimony to the plain teaching of historical facts on the latter.

A translation of the very important work upon Anglican Orders by V. Sokoloff, Professor of Ecclesiastical History in the Academy of Moscow, which is referred to several times in the course of this article, is now in preparation under the auspices of the Church Historical Society, and will shortly appear.

W. E. COLLINS.

SUMMARY.

—◦—

THE QUESTION OF ANGLICAN ORDERS.

—•—

INTRODUCTION.

DURING the last five years one of the largest and most important questions which the representatives of theological science have had to deal with has been the question of the Anglican hierarchy. So numerous have been the works devoted to its discussion by scholars and publicists in England, Italy, France, and Russia, that a mere list of them would form a pamphlet of considerable dimensions. The reason that the question has attracted so much attention lies in the fact that upon its solution in one direction or the other depends the solution of the further question as to what Anglicanism essentially is, and what are its relations towards those Christian confessions of faith which look upon the Church's hierarchy as a Divine institution which must of necessity exist in unbroken order of succession in the Church of Christ in every period of her existence—that is to say, to the end of the world—and therefore as an institution without which the very existence of the Church of Christ is impossible.

The question concerning the Anglican hierarchy arose at the very commencement of its existence [1]—that is to say, in the sixteenth century, when the question as to its relations with Roman Catholicism had to be settled ; but, strange as it may seem, no satisfactory solution was found through the course of three centuries ; indeed, it may be said that even up to the present time it has not been settled satisfactorily or finally. We have no intention of giving a detailed history of the attempts that have been made to settle it, our desire rather is to acquaint the readers of our journal with the exact position of the question at the present time.

[1] [си, that is, the existence of the hierarchy. W. J. B.]

For all representatives of those forms of Christianity which are interested in a final solution of the question of the Anglican hierarchy, this question falls under two divisions: the historico-canonical, and the dogmatic [sides of the matter]. The first of these may be formulated thus:—"Does the present Anglican hierarchy possess an immediate connexion with the Apostolic hierarchy?"—or in other words: "Has a laying on of hands of uninterrupted apostolical succession been preserved in it?" The second half of the question presents itself in the following aspect:— "Does the Anglican hierarchy of the present day possess those indispensable properties and qualities, without which the existence of the hierarchy according to the mind of its Divine Founder is an impossibility?" Or: "Is the Anglican hierarchy of the present day what it ought to be from the point of view of Holy Scripture and Holy Tradition?" Each of these divisions of the question is of such a nature, that a negative solution of even one of them must lead to the denial of the significance of the hierarchy in Anglicanism and would, so to speak, be the pronouncement of a death-warrant upon Anglicanism itself, inasmuch as it would reduce it to the level of a Protestant sect[1]. It was just such a sentence upon Anglicanism that the representatives of Roman Catholicism had in view to pronounce when they tried to prove that Matthew Parker, Archbishop of Canterbury, the source of the Anglican hierarchy[2], had not received consecration from persons possessed of an unbroken chain of episcopal succession deriving its origin from the Apostles, and that, therefore, the Anglican hierarchy had not the apostolical succession. In order as far as possible to minimize the significance of Parker as a bishop, a monstrous and absurd fable was concocted to the effect that the whole order of his consecration had been a profane ceremony, which took place not even in a church, but in one of the London taverns. Thus the Roman Catholics from the earliest times of the

---

[1] The Anglican Archbishops themselves take this view of the significance of this question, when they say in their Reply to the Bull of Leo XIII that "there suddenly arrived in this country from Rome a letter . . . which aimed at overthrowing our whole position as a Church."—*Answer of the Archbishops of England*, § 1.

[2] [Of course, Parker is not the only "source of the Anglican hierarchy." As is well known, the Irish and Dalmatian successions were united with the English in the consecration of William Laud as Bishop of St. Davids. (Denny and Lacey, *De Hierarchia Anglicana*, App. I.) W. E. C.]

existence of the Anglican hierarchy solved the historico-canonical side of the question in a negative sense, that is to say, they denied that this hierarchy had any real significance, inasmuch as it did not possess an uninterrupted connexion with the Apostolic hierarchy; whilst in the case of any of its members passing over to Roman Catholicism, they considered it necessary to reordain them to the various degrees of the hierarchy, beginning with the lowest. It ought, however, to be said that such cases were few in number, and accordingly did not produce a great impression: with respect to each of them a special arrangement was made, but no general decision binding upon all Roman Catholics was pronounced by Rome. The silence of Pius IX upon this matter seems particularly strange and difficult to account for; for in general he was decided in his opinions and actions, and moreover he had good reasons for making a pronouncement upon Anglicanism[1]. This pronouncement was not, however, made until two years ago, namely, in the Bull of Pope Leo XIII of September 1 (13), 1896. According to the sentence pronounced in this Bull, the Anglican hierarchy has no significance whatever (it is " null " and " void "). In view of the previous relations of Roman Catholicism towards Anglicanism, the judgement of the Pope cannot be said to be anything but what was to be expected, and the importance of the Bull *Apostolicae Curae,* as far as theological science is concerned, consists, not in the sentence therein pronounced, but rather in the processes employed by the Pope in order to prove his main point. He quite rightly defined the significance of the actions of one of his predecessors (Clement XI) by pointing out the fact that this Pope had based his decision concerning the Anglican hierarchy, not upon the ground of historico-canonical data, but upon the ground of the nature of the Anglican Order of Ordination. Following the example of his predecessor, Pope Leo XIII introduces historico-canonical material into the Bull only by way of reference, and is principally concerned with the settlement of the dogmatic side of the question ; but he also decides it in a negative sense. Accordingly, by the sentence of the Pope—a sentence pronounced *ex cathedra*[2]—the Anglican hierarchy is declared to

---

[1] Pius IX established the hierarchy of the Roman Catholics in England.

[2] [We are nowhere definitely told so, but the Pope himself speaks of his decision as "firmam, ratam, irrevocabilem," and many Roman Catholics speak of it as infallible. (See *Priesthood in the English Church,* p. 15 note.) It

have no significance for Roman Catholics, and to be null; that is to say, Anglicanism in the eyes of the Roman Catholics has been finally and irreversibly reduced to the level of a Protestant sect. By the Pope's command the Bull itself may neither be "impugned" nor "objected to"; and no one may attempt anything against it.

Six months after the Bull saw the light—that is to say, on Feb. 19, 1897—the Primate of the Anglican Church, the Archbishop of Canterbury, together with the other Anglican Archbishop (of York), published a *Responsio* or "Answer" to the Pope's Bull in Latin and in English [1]. Thus, whilst, according to the calculations of the Roman Catholics, the decision which it contained had to be regarded as indisputable and absolute, the Pope's Bull was made the subject of serious criticism on the part of the defenders of the Anglican hierarchy. We will not give the contents of this criticism here at length. We will merely observe that upon all the questions touched upon by the Bull, the Anglican Archbishops expressed their opinion perfectly clearly and definitely, and that they subjected to a thorough criticism the practice of the Roman Catholic Church in relation to Anglican ordinations in the few instances pointed out by the Pope. They applied themselves to the defence of the Anglican order of the laying on of hands on those points against which the Pope had raised objections. So that, if the contents of Leo XIII's Bull of Sept. 1 (13), 1896, be compared with the contents of the Anglican Archbishops' reply of February 7 (19), 1897, one may be quite clearly satisfied that, in spite of the lengthy and careful investigations of the Roman Catholic commission which Leo XIII appointed for the purpose, no documents were to be found in the Roman archives which could serve as a justification of the Roman Catholic practice in respect to Anglicanism, or as a solid ground for a definite solution of the historico-canonical side of the question of Anglican Orders. Indeed, Pope Leo XIII feels the precariousness [*lit.* shakiness] of the historico-canonical ground beneath him, and therefore passes on to the solving of the dogmatic side of the question. But in this respect

may be doubted, however, whether the Bull would satisfy the conditions laid down by Ballerini, *De Potest. Eccl.* App. *de infallib.*, or De Bartolo, *Les Critères Théologiques*, chap. iii. W. E. C.]

[1] Those who wish to acquaint themselves with this "Answer" in its complete form can find it in *The Theological Messenger*, June and July, 1897; while it appears in a shortened form in *The Orthodox Speaker*, May, 1897, pp. 705–26.

the contemporary Roman Order of laying on of hands itself, according to the well-grounded observation of the Anglican Archbishops, turns out to have a great number of defects; so that to establish a final solution of the question of the validity of the Anglican episcopal hierarchy, with only this Order as a guide, is impossible. In a word, " Rome had spoken," but the matter turned out not to have been ended, inasmuch as in the Pope's decision there were found to be no small number of historico-canonical and liturgical blunders; so that there seemed some danger that the Pope's Bull might lose its significance even in the eyes of the Roman Catholics, and instead of benefiting them might do them injury. And such an injury was especially to be feared in England. In order to weaken as far as possible—even if they could not entirely get rid of—the unpleasant consequences which might arise from such a turn of affairs and to forestall the evil which might result therefrom, it was found necessary to undertake the defence of the Bull *Apostolicae Curae.* This defence the English Roman Catholic Bishops took upon themselves; they, with Cardinal Vaughan at their head, having been, according to the opinion of many people, responsible for the Bull having seen the light[1]. At the end of last year they put forth a pamphlet: "*A Vindication of the Bull 'Apostolicae Curae.' A Letter on Anglican Orders.* By the Cardinal-Archbishop and the Bishops of the Province of Westminster. London, New York, and Bombay. 1898." This pamphlet is of great importance in the controversy concerning Anglican Ordinations, because in it the question is decided from a new point of view which was scarcely touched upon in the Bull, and was passed over almost in silence in the criticisms contained in the reply of the Anglican Archbishops.

---

[1] See V. Sokoloff's work on the *Hierarchy of the Anglican Episcopal Church,* pp. 151-5, where many extracts are quoted from the English periodicals from articles which appeared after the publication of the Bull in England, and which are devoted to its discussion. But this idea appeared earlier still in our periodical press. See *Transactions of the Kieff Eccl. Acad.* June, 1895, p. 342.

I.

The *Vindication of the Bull "Apostolicae Curae"* consists of fifty short sections (including the introduction and conclusion) and eight appendices which are necessary for the clearer understanding of the text. In the introduction (§ 1) the authors of the *Vindication* say that, as representatives of Roman Catholicism in England, they consider it necessary to call the attention of the Most Reverend Lord Archbishops of the English Church to their misunderstanding both of the motives for which the Bull was published, and also of the grounds upon which the Papal decision upon the question of Anglican orders is based : the greater part of their argument is grounded upon this very misunderstanding of the Bull. What the authors of the *Vindication* wish to do is to explain the real meaning of the Bull; and at the same time they comfort themselves with the thought that they [i. e. the Archbishops] will not suspect them of any desire of gaining a controversial victory in the discussion upon the given subject. The *Vindication* then begins (§ 2) by the affirmation of the idea that in the Church of Christ there must be a supreme authority for deciding questions of faith ; to this authority belongs the right of passing a final judgement upon the elementary, vital, and practical question as to such an administration of the Sacraments as shall assure their validity. Such an indisputable authority must be recognized in the Pope; without this authority unimaginable confusion will spring up in the Church founded by Jesus Christ ; to deny such an authority is tantamount to striking at the very roots of the Sacramental system. The Bull *Apostolicae Curae* was written (§ 3) with the object of guarding against the risk (*a*) of a sacrilegious reiteration of the Sacrament of Orders on the one hand, and (*b*) of invalid administration of it on the other. Certain Anglicans [1] had urged the Roman See to make

---

[1] That is to say, the Ritualists, from amongst whom Lord Halifax actually entered into personal relations with the Pope with a view to clearing up the causes of division between Roman Catholicism and Anglicanism, and, if possible, co-operating in removing them. *Transactions*, 1895, No. 6, p. 343, and No. 12, pp. 680-1. Sokoloff, *op. cit.*, pp. 127-8.

a new investigation of this question, and the Bull was published with a view to satisfying their desire ; in it the Pope only sets forth the results of a careful and impartial investigation carried out by a distinguished commission, and puts a limit to various mischievous opinions ; he did it in a spirit of peace, and was guided by a hearty goodwill towards the English people. But inasmuch as the Anglicans suspected the impartiality of the results of the Roman Catholic inquiries into the question of the Anglican hierarchy, (§ 4) the Roman Catholic Bishops in England have decided once more to go over this matter in order to convince the Anglicans that their objections to the Bull are unfounded.

(§ 6) The Anglicans in their *Answer* to the Papal Bull do not admit the argument of the Pope based upon the practice of Rome in relation to Anglican Orders to be of serious importance, although it is extremely natural that a tribunal, when any matter is brought before it for investigation, should carefully inquire into its past decisions in like cases. Next (§§ 7, 8) the Roman Catholic Bishops pass to the discussion of those pieces of historical evidence which were brought forward by the Pope as references concerning the previous practice of Rome in relation to Anglicanism. This prac- tice shows that at the time of the Roman Catholic reaction under Queen Mary some of the clergy who had been ordained according to the new Ordinal drawn up in the reign of Edward VI, were either reordained according to the Roman Catholic Ordinal, or were deposed in consequence of the *nullity of their previous ordination,* and that this settlement had been arrived at on the ground of an examination of the Order of Ordination which had been drawn up under Edward VI to take the place of the Roman Catholic Ordinal. An examination of this Order also took place in the year 1704, when the case of J. Gordon, an Anglican Bishop who had gone over to Roman Catholicism, had to be settled. This is proved by the fact that when the case of J. Gordon was settled, there were documents, of the authenticity of which there can be no doubt, which make it evident that the decree of Pope Clement XI was based upon the lack in the Anglican Order of Ordination (*a*) of an entirely precise definition of the degree in the hierarchy to which the Ordinand was to be raised, and (*b*) of the distinguishing nature of each of the degrees of holy orders.

Passing on (§ 9) to the principal part of the Bull, the authors of the *Vindication* point out that the main object of the Pope

was, not the opening of an inquiry into the Roman Catholic doctrines of the sacrifice and the priesthood, but the determination
whether, or *to what degree*, the Anglican Ordinal fulfils certain
conditions, without which, according to the doctrine of the Roman
Catholics, it is absolutely impossible to acknowledge a priesthood
or episcopate to be what they claim to be. Next, having pointed
out (§ 10) that the doctrines of the Real Presence of Jesus Christ
in the Sacrament of the Eucharist, the Eucharistic Sacrifice, and of
the Priesthood are so intimately connected, that this fact must
of necessity find expression in the distinguishing features of the
order of laying on of hands, the English Roman Catholic Bishops
devote the next four sections (§§ 11–14) to an exposition of the
doctrine of the Roman Catholic Church as to the Real Presence
of Jesus Christ in the Eucharist, the Eucharist as the Sacrifice
of the Cross [1], of the Priesthood, as the sacrificial service of the
New Covenant [2], that is to say, a service of which the distinguishing
peculiarity consists in the offering the bloodless sacrifice of the New
Testament, and, lastly, they expound their teaching concerning
Transubstantiation. "Priest and Sacrifice are correlative terms.
A priest is one who offers sacrifice." This is the opinion of all
nations. A priest may also have other powers from God, for
instance, he may have the power of forgiving sins, of teaching,
and exercising pastoral care; but these are superadded powers:
they are only annexed to the priesthood, but are not of its essence.
Agreeably with the dogmas here set forth we find further on (§ 15)
those peculiar features defined which are the essentials of an
Ordinal. Accordingly, we must regard this, the fifteenth section of
the *Vindication*, to be the doctrine of the Roman Catholics upon the
Sacrament of Orders from the dogmatic point of view in its applica-

---

[1] [*Sic.* объ евхаристіи, какъ крестной жертвѣ. But he clearly means
"of the Eucharist in its relation to the Sacrifice of the Cross." W. J. B.]

[2] [жреческомъ новозавѣтномъ служеніи. With respect to the word
жреческомъ (sacrificial), the author has a foot-note, in which he says:] It is
true that this term [жреческомъ] is not employed, but the ideas of *sacerdotium*
and *sacerdotalis* correspond completely to the ideas concerning the priesthood
which are expressed in the *Vindication*. See pages 50, 51, and 46, where
sacerdotium, *sacerdos*, and *summus sacerdos* are used. [The reason that he
apologizes for the use of the word is that the word жрецъ is used in ordinary
Russian of *heathen* priesthoods, and in the Church language (Old Slavonic)
of the *Old Testament* priesthood, but never, in either language, of the *Christian*
priesthood. W. J. B.]

tion to the Order for the laying on of hands. The essence of this doctrine, as set forth in this section, is as follows. Our Lord in instituting the Christian priesthood, determined that it should be perpetuated through the ages by means of an Apostolical Succession, that is to say, that it should be continued from age to age by its transmission from generation to generation. Accordingly, nobody possesses either a valid priesthood, or a valid episcopate, unless he has received the same through a succession from the Apostles. But, on the other hand, no one, except the Lord Jesus Christ Himself, could annex the power of communicating a gift so stupendous to a certain sacramental rite. Only from the unfailing tradition of the Roman Catholic Church can we derive our knowledge as to the necessary elements of the outward circumstances of a valid Ordination. On the outward side of the administration of each of the Sacraments, it is necessary to distinguish the essential and indispensable part from that which is purely ceremonial. The essential part is short, and in most of the Sacraments very short; it must (*a*) indicate clearly, and not ambiguously, the grace or power which is to be conveyed in the Sacrament; (*b*) it must [in the Sacrament of Orders] define the gift of the grace of the priesthood in its distinction from the gifts of grace bestowed in other Sacraments. On the other side, in accordance with Christ's institution, in every sacrament two elements must be distinguished; (*a*) a series of actions attached to the Sacrament, which since the twelfth or thirteenth century have been usually called the *matter*, and (*b*) an accompanying form of words, which has usually been called the *form* in the more restricted sense of this word[1]; having this in view, the definiteness of the signification of the Sacrament must be chiefly sought *in the form*, since the words *of the form* are able to define the meaning with precision, whilst external actions without the words which accompany them can hardly be without ambiguity. Accordingly it is necessary to recognize, that either the matter or the form, or one and the other together, were prescribed by our Lord himself *in specie*, and not merely *in genere*. Accordingly to look upon the imposition of hands as the *matter* of the Sacrament of Orders is impossible; for it by itself signifies nothing definite,

---

[1] The various significations of the word *form* as applied to a sacrament are pointed out by the authors in a foot-note on pp. 31, 32. A *form* is either (*a*) the whole sacramental rite, or (*b*) its principal part, or (*c*) the words which actually accomplish the Sacrament.

and is indiscriminately used for various degrees of the priesthood and even for Confirmation; therefore in the examination of the rite for Holy Orders we must look to the question: *do the words which accompany the imposition of hands definitely signify or express that grace or power which is conveyed in the Sacrament of Orders, that is to say, the power of consecrating and offering in sacrifice the true Body and true Blood of the Lord in that priestly action which is no nude commemoration of the sacrifice of the Cross?* Having expounded the teaching of their church as to the essential part of the Order of laying on of hands, the Roman Catholic Bishops pass on to the exposition of their teaching *concerning the intention* of the minister of the Sacrament (§ 16). According to this teaching, *in order that the Sacrament may be valid the minister must have the intention to do what the Church wished or wishes to do.* The intention is considered to be sufficiently manifested, if the minister have rightly and seriously performed all the outward part of the rite which is accessible to the senses [1], as the Bull says.

Relying upon the above reasonings, the authors of the *Vindication* pass on to the assertion of the notion that Anglican Ordinations can in no respect be recognized as sufficient, that is to say, as corresponding to what they claim to be (§ 17); and in the following sections (§§ 18–22) they review the Anglican Ordinal from the three points of view indicated by the Bull *Apostolicae curae*: (*a*) from the point of view of the insufficiency of the essential part; (*b*) from the point of view of the insufficiency of the rite as a whole, and (*c*) from the point of view of the want of due intention, in so far as it is displayed in the rite. They begin their investigation of the Anglican Ordinal with the question of intention, and settle it very simply: the Anglican rite for Holy Orders shows that the intention of the Anglican minister does not correspond with the intention of the Roman Catholic Church, and consequently annuls the force of the Sacrament. With regard to the words in the Anglican Ordinal, which [are intended to] accomplish the Sacrament, the *Vindication* says, that neither the form of 1552, nor yet the additions to it, made in 1662, are sufficient for the validity of the Sacrament of Orders: in these forms the priesthood is not indicated as being

---

[1] In his Bull the Pope goes so far as to advance the notion that a Sacrament is valid even if it be performed by a heretic or unbaptized man, provided only that it be performed according to the Roman Catholic rite—that is to say, he carries the doctrine of *opus operatum* to the furthest point.

the sacerdotal ministry of the New Covenant, for there is no mention of the power to offer the bloodless sacrifice of the New Covenant; and moreover in the Order for the Consecration of a Bishop there is nothing to express the difference of the office of a bishop from that of a priest. The authors of the *Vindication* have brought forward nothing new in proof of their assertions, and nothing which was not already to be found in the papal Bull, except it be that they point out a contradiction, which in its essence is of no importance, in the Anglican reply to the Bull.

The following three sections (§§ 23–25) are directed against those objections of the Anglicans which insist upon the fact that the *forms* of the ancient ordination rites which have come down to us have not a fully defined character, and that national churches have the right to introduce their own *forms* for these rites. The Roman Catholics first reply to the second half of this objection. The essence of their answer amounts simply to this: in acknowledging the "decrees" of the Word of God, and of "the known and certain statutes of the Universal Church," the Anglicans ought to have arrived at the conclusion that they must not omit or reform anything in these forms which immemorial tradition has bequeathed to us. Roman Catholicism, according to the testimony of one of the authorities upon the Roman Pontifical [1], treats the matter thus: the present Roman Pontifical contains all that was in the earlier Pontificals, but the earlier Pontificals do not contain all that is in the modern one. National churches allowed themselves to make additions of prayers and ceremonies—of this there is no doubt— but to shorten or seriously to modify or alter rites was not permitted, and seems [to them] to be something incredible; so that the English Reformers (Cranmer) in this instance acted with an unwarranted and unpraiseworthy rashness. The assertion too that the ancient forms of Ordination were indefinite and dissimilar is untrue. The Papal Bull does not require that the *form* of the Sacrament should consist in all cases of one and the same verbal expressions, but merely requires that it should agree with one and the same definite and universally acknowledged type: the *form* must definitely express the sacred Order of the priesthood or episcopate, *or* its grace and power, which consists chiefly of the power of consecrating and offering the Body and Blood of the Lord. Having explained that in the Roman Catholic Church the terms

---

[1] Morinus, *De sacris ordinationibus* [pars iii. p. 10. W. E. C.]

"priest" (*presbyter*) and "bishop" or "high priest" have always
been used in the sense of persons bearing the aforesaid grace and
possessing the above-named powers (§ 26), the Roman Catholics
call attention to the fact that in the Anglican Church, on the
contrary, these terms have not the meanings which are attached
to them by both Eastern and Western Christians (§ 27). Although
the *forms* of the administration of the Sacrament of Orders of
these are different, they nevertheless all suggest the idea of the
priesthood as the *sacerdotium*[1] of the New Testament. The
English Reformers, on the contrary, having retained the names
of the various grades of the hierarchy, applied to them only their
etymological meaning[2], and expressed the wish that henceforth
those ordained should be regarded, not as ministers empowered
to offer sacrifice, but merely as pastors, teachers, administrators of
the Sacraments (in the Anglican sense of the word) and in general
as spiritual guardians. In the two following sections (§§ 28, 29)
defects in the Anglican rite as a whole are pointed out; in it not
only are there no prayers which speak of a true priesthood, but,
on the contrary, the prayers of this kind, which existed in the
Anglican Ordinals before the Reformation, have been carefully
altered or eliminated, so that from the present Anglican rite every
trace of ideas concerning sacrifice, consecration, the priesthood,
and of power to consecrate and offer sacrifice, is blotted out (§ 30).
The silence of the Anglican rite on the subjects here named must
be laid to the blame of the Reformers, for they were silent as
to *what* in the rite of Ordination *must indispensably be retained*
as its essential and integral part. In the Anglican rite of Ordination there is a long series of questions which are put to the
candidates about to be ordained, and not one of these questions
mentions the consecration of the sacrifice. On the other hand
the outlines of a Protestant pastorate are clearly indicated. Moreover, the Roman Catholics say that they are comparing the
Anglican Ordinal, not with the most ancient and simple forms

---

[1] [жречество. This word is (like жрець, vide p. 16 note 2) used only in
respect to the Old Testament or a heathen priesthood, in distinction to священство,
the Christian priesthood, which is here translated "priesthood." W. J. B.]

[2] *A Vindication*, p. 48. In proof of their statement the authors of the
Vindication quote an extract from Hooker's *Ecclesiastical Polity*, v. 78, § 3:
"Seeing, then, that sacrifice is now no part of the Church ministry, how should
the name of priesthood be thereunto rightly applied?" &c.

of the Roman Catholic rite, but with those mediaeval rites which were in use at the time of the so-called Reformation. Corresponding omissions and changes were made by the English Reformers in the Order of the administration of the Eucharist, that is to say, the idea of a true sacrifice and a real *objective* presence of Jesus Christ in the Sacrament were excluded (§ 31). Can there be any doubt that all the intentions of the composers both of the English Ordinal and of the English prayer-book were directed to that end? Cranmer must be regarded as their principal author—he was the highest ecclesiastical authority at that time—and their contents must be judged of, not by those explanations favourable to Catholicism, which some assign to them, but by the views of Cranmer (§ 33), who was not only one of the principal compilers of the new forms of service, but the principal actor in getting them through Parliament in spite of the opposition of those Bishops that did not agree with Cranmer's views. Further sections (§§ 34-36) of the *Vindication* are devoted to an exposition of Cranmer's views. With this object the authors of the *Vindication* make extracts out of some of Cranmer's writings [1], which show that he rejected the doctrine of the real presence of Jesus Christ in the Sacrament of the Eucharist, and of the Eucharist as a Sacrifice, speaking of such dogmas as anti-Christian inventions of Popery, and declared that Jesus Christ did not appoint such a distinction between the priest and the layman, as that a priest should have power to offer sacrifice for the layman, and God did not give a promise of grace for the ecclesiastical office in greater measure than for the civil office. The same was taught by Cranmer's colleagues and contemporaries, Ridley, Barlow, Ferrar, Goodrich, Coverdale, Taylor (§ 37, and Appendix). And they set forth their views in their deeds, in the destruction of altars and the substitution for them of simple tables, for, as they said, "the use of an altar is to make sacrifice upon it, the use of a table is to serve men to eat upon it" (§ 38), and in general "the form of a simple table shall more move the simple from the superstitious opinions of the Popish Mass unto the right use of the Lord's Supper" (§ 38). Moreover, those of the Anglican Articles of Religion which concern the doctrine of the Eucharist, namely

---

[1] *A defence of the True and Catholic Doctrine concerning the sacrament of the Body and Blood of Christ,* and also his reply to the questions of Henry VIII in 1540.

Articles 28, 29, and 31, are drawn up agreeably with the views of these theologians (§ 39). Even if Cranmer does use the terms "real presence," "sacrifice," "priesthood," he uses them in a metaphorical, figurative sense ; and these terms are employed in a similar manner by other (later) Anglican divines (§§ 40-43, and App. III), as a conspicuous example of which may be mentioned Waterland, a theologian of the eighteenth century (§ 44). And it is only latterly in recent times that a return may be seen to the true doctrine of the Eucharist and the priesthood, as in his time Newman testified (§ 45).

And so, the authors of the *Vindication* of the Papal Bull conclude, up to a certain point the Anglican Church, if we may judge from the teaching of her principal divines, has a doctrine both of a sacrifice and of a priesthood; but they understand sacrifice and priesthood, not as do the Roman Catholics in a literal, but only in a metaphorical sense. But resemblances must not be confounded with realities : "the true Sacrifice and Priesthood—that is to say, the Sacrifice in which the true Body and Blood of Christ is sacrificed and offered, and the Priesthood which is endowed with power to consecrate and offer it—your Church has repudiated altogether." And (§ 46) it is just this that the Bull of Leo XIII asserts. The teaching of the present Anglican Archbishops upon these subjects seems to the authors of the *Vindication* to agree entirely with the teaching of Cranmer, his colleagues, and the later Anglican divines (§ 47); and accordingly they ask the Anglican Archbishops to state directly, clearly, and definitely whether their teaching has been rightly understood by the Pope and other Roman Catholics with regard to these crucial points (§ 48) upon which the great Churches of the East teach exactly the same as the Roman Catholic Church (§ 49 and App. VII).

In the concluding section (§ 50) the authors of the *Vindication* turn to the concluding words of the Anglican *Responsio* to the Papal Bull, and say that they are able to subscribe to that part of their (the Anglican Archbishops') reply in which they express their desire for peace and unity in the Church. But in this respect Roman Catholics go beyond them. They firmly hold the doctrine that *the visible unity* of the Church is of the very essence of her being, and not merely of her well-being; they bewail the sad spectacle of divisions among Christians, and recognize it to be opposed to the revealed purpose of God. They agree that it is very important to be guided by personal and national tastes and proclivities, but only under the condition of constantly turning towards our Lord Jesus Christ and weighing patiently what He intended when He established the ministry of His Gospel. "Oh! that the happy day might come when you could be in accord with us also in perceiving that the secret of visible unity is to be sought, not in the system which during its comparatively short-lived existence has been the fertile mother of division, but rather in that system which has stood firm through the ages, holding the nations together in a unity so conspicuous as to excite admiration even where it fails to secure obedience!" The *Vindication* is signed by the Cardinal Archbishop of Westminster, Herbert Vaughan, and the fifteen Bishops of the Roman Catholic Church in England. It was published on the day of (St.) Thomas [1], Archbishop of Canterbury (Dec. 29), the well-known champion of the secular power of the Pope against the English King Henry II, who by the Roman Catholics is numbered amongst the martyrs.

In the Appendices to the *Vindication* the Roman Catholic Bishops examine more minutely those documents which in the Bull *Apostolicae Curae* were only briefly expounded or touched upon, adding some new ones either in their entirety or in the form of extracts. (I) Expressions are quoted from the letter of Julius III to Cardinal Pole of March 8, 1554, in which it is betokened in general outlines that the Cardinal may freely make use of the authority of the Apostolic See in what he did. Nothing is said here about Ordination, and it is difficult to conceive—if we are to judge from the words which are quoted from it in the *Vindication* —what connexion this document has with the question of Anglican Orders. Of this we shall speak more in detail further on. (II) An extract is quoted from the decree of Eugenius IV in respect to the Armenians. In this decree the Pope recognizes as the *matter* of the Sacrament not the laying on of hands, but the porrection of the "instruments" of service: to the priest a chalice with wine and a paten with bread, and to the deacon the book of the Gospels. The words "Receive the power of offering sacrifice in the Church for the living and the dead" are recognized as the *form* of the Sacrament. This is an extremely important document, and the Roman Catholics devote a considerable space to an explanation of it.

---

[1] [въ день (св) Ооми. W. J. B.]

(III) The decision of Clement XI in 1704 in respect to Abyssinian Ordinations is considered. Clement XI did not agree with the opinion of one of the consultors that the ordination of a deacon by means of the imposition of the patriarchal cross and the negligent Ordination of presbyters was not valid, and propounded the resolution, *Dilata ad mentem,* that is to say it is referred to the number of private opinions. This question is also extremely important, and the authors of the *Vindication* bring forward a great many considerations in order to account for this fact. (IV) A comparison is made of prayers pronounced at the moment of Ordination, in the older forms of Ordination—that is to say, the Roman Order according to the Sacramentary of Leo I, the Greek, the Maronite, the Nestorian, the Armenian, the Coptic, the Abyssinian, the Old Gallican, the Apostolic Constitutions, and the so-called Canons of Hippolytus. The extracts from the prayers are quoted without commentary with the object of proving that in each of the aforesaid rites (which the Roman Catholic Church acknowledges as valid) there is a mention of the degree in the hierarchy to which the Ordinand is being raised, and the character of the powers bestowed upon him is more or less indicated. (V) and (VI) A number of extracts are given from the writings of various Anglican divines concerning the Sacraments of the Eucharist and Orders. (VII). An English translation follows of the seventeenth Article of the *Epistle of the Eastern Patriarchs concerning the Faith* [1], in order to show that the doctrine of the Orthodox Church concerning the Sacrament of the Eucharist does not agree with that of the Anglicans. (VIII) The literature upon the subject of Anglican Orders is mentioned. Out of the multitude of separate works which have appeared upon the subject, the Roman Catholics mention only *ten,* and these written by Roman Catholic writers.

---

[1] The *Vindication* calls this *Epistle* the Decrees of the Council of Bethlehem, 1672, concerning the Eucharist (vide pp. 116-21). In the *Epistle* itself this Council is called the Council of Jerusalem. Vide *The Imperial and Patriarchal Letters with the Exposition of the Orthodox Confession of Faith.* St. Petersburg, 1838.

II.

The work of the Roman Catholic Bishops of England which we have just been examining was sent to the Anglican Archbishops, and they did not delay to give their answer [which appeared] in the form of a short letter on March 12, 1898 [1]. In this reply the Anglican Archbishops say that they have carefully and attentively read the *Vindication of the Bull "Apostolicae Curae,"* and have found nothing new in it. They refuse to acknowledge the pretensions of the Pope to ascendency and unconditional authority, just as the great Churches of the East very sensibly do. The chaos with which the Roman Catholics threaten Christian communities, who do not acknowledge the supremacy of the Pope, is as a matter of fact not in the least noticeable there. They assign an extremely small polemical importance to the production of the Roman Catholics, for the *Vindication* for the most part is concerned, not with the question of Orders, but of the relation of the Sacrament of the Eucharist to Orders. If the question had been put in this way, then, say the Archbishops, "our answer must have taken a different form. But we could not answer what he did not say." Cardinal Vaughan places the validity of Orders in direct connexion with the recognition of the doctrine of Transubstantiation. The view taken by the Anglican Church of the Roman Catholic doctrine of Transubstantiation she has already long ago exactly stated, and the Archbishops sincerely accept what that part of Article XXVIII of their Church says upon the subject. "It is, for us," they further say, "simply impossible to believe it to be the will of our Lord that admission to the ministry of the Church of Christ should depend upon the acceptance of a metaphysical definition, expressed in terms of mediaeval philosophy, of the mysterious gift bestowed in the Holy Eucharist." Such a doctrine was unknown to the Church in the

---

[1] *The Anglican Archbishops' Reply to Cardinal Vaughan.* This reply was signed only by F. Cantuar. (Frederick of Canterbury) and Willelm. Ebor. (William of York), that is to say, the Archbishops of the Anglican Church.

first ages of her existence, and was generally diffused only after its assertion by the Roman Church in the thirteenth century. The letter concludes by a prayer to God for the reunion of all Christians, and by the expression of sincere regret that the chief hindrance to reunion appears to be, on the one hand, the pretensions of the Pope to supremacy and infallibility, and, on the other hand, the new dogmas which from time to time are accepted by the Roman Church.

Such an answer as this to the Roman Catholic *Vindication* of Leo XIII's Bull evidently is in substance a refusal on the part of the Anglican Archbishops to continue an official correspondence and controversy with Cardinal Vaughan and the English Roman Catholic Bishops. And apparently the latter take the reply of the Anglicans as such. But in as much as the Anglicans from the beginning of the controversy on the question of the Orders of their Church endeavoured to attract the attention of Orthodox theologians (Russian and Greek) to the matter with a view to hearing the opinion of the authoritative representatives of ecclesiastical and theological spheres of the Orthodox Church (in which they succeeded to a certain degree), so the representatives of Roman Catholicism in England likewise considered it indispensable to follow the example of the Anglican Archbishops. The Anglican Archbishops wrote their *Answer* to the Papal Bull with the object of submitting it [the Bull] [1] to the judgement of *all the Bishops of the Universal Church* [2], and sent it [the *Responsio*] [3] direct to them immediately

---

[1] [сл, genitive feminine to agree with бұллы, understood. W. J. B.]

[2] The *Answer* to the Bull is addressed " to the whole Body of Bishops of the Catholic Church." Even before this the Anglicans had endeavoured to interest Russian theologians in the question of Anglican Orders by the distribution in Russia of a book, *De hierarchia Anglicana*, by Denny and Lacey. Amongst others, I received a copy of this book ; to a certain degree it may be regarded as an official work, drawn up in defence of the Anglican hierarchy, inasmuch as its contents were sanctioned by episcopal authority : its Preface was written by John Wordsworth, Bishop of Salisbury (Sarum). This is what he writes : " Commendo ergo *lectoribus externis* opus quod sequitur : probatum iam in Anglia, et Latina versione iam merito donatum, *ut plenius et accuratius in orbem christianum procedat.*" Praefatio, p. x. The consequence of this endeavour to interest Russian theologians was a whole series of articles in the Russian ecclesiastical journal, and a separate monograph by V. Sokoloff devoted to the question of Anglican Orders.

[3] [его, genitive masculine, agreeing with отвѣта, understood. W. J. B.]

after its publication, requesting them at the end of it to "join [with them] in weighing patiently what Christ intended when He established the ministry of His Gospel." Cardinal Vaughan did the same thing on behalf of his Bishops in England. At the end of last June he put forth a letter in the English and Russian languages, which he sent to Russia, together with copies of his *Vindication* and the above-described short reply of the Anglican Archbishops. I also had the opportunity of making the acquaintance of one of these copies of the *Vindication*, the Anglican reply to it, and Cardinal Vaughan's accompanying letter.

In this accompanying letter the Cardinal indicates as follows the reason for publishing the *Vindication*, and for sending it to Russia: "We have heard that this question of Anglican Orders excites a good deal of interest in Russia, and as the Letter of the Anglican Archbishops was sent to you, we thought that you might like to have also our *Vindication of the Papal Bull.*" . . . "We send it the more readily because it is our consolation to know you are as solicitous as we are in guarding not only the Apostolic Succession of Orders, but also the Roman Catholic (католическихъ), doctrines of the Priesthood, of Transubstantiation (пресуществленіи) [1], of the Real Presence, and of the Sacrifice of the Mass; so that you are in a position to appreciate with clearness and accuracy the force of arguments based on the right understanding of these doctrines." After which follows a short description of the last Anglican reply, and it is pointed out that the *Vindication* in its line of argument follows in all respects the direction indicated by the Pope's Bull. Cardinal Vaughan concludes his letter with the desire that the truth may be known, preserved, and defended, and that in the knowledge of the truth " we may all be drawn more and more nearly to one another." The letter is signed by Cardinal Vaughan himself (*Herbert Cardinal Vaughan, Archbishop of Westminster*) on the Feast of the Holy Apostles Peter and Paul,

---

[1] [Professor Bulgakoff has not made use of the Russian version provided by Cardinal Vaughan, but has throughout made a fresh translation from the English text. This is the only place, however, where the variation is noteworthy. Cardinal Vaughan translates *Transubstantiation* by трансусбстанціацін, whereas Professor Bulgakoff uses the Orthodox terminology, and writes пресуществленіе, which corresponds, not to *transubstantiatio*, but to μετουσίωσις. W. J. B.]

that is, on the 17th (29th) of June, 1898, at Archbishop's House, London[1].

This is the last document which has appeared up to this time in the official controversy on the question of Anglican Orders. Let us now see to what deductions we may arrive at on the basis of this controversy.

[1] [A facsimile of this letter, as it was received by the Russian metropolitans, is added as an appendix to the present translation ; since it is the only document which has hitherto been unknown to English readers.   W. E. C.]

III.

The whole of Leo XIII's Bull, if we lay aside its introduction and its conclusion, may be represented in the following general aspect: Anglican Ordinations cannot be acknowledged to be valid, because (*a*) they are conferred *according to a form* which does not correspond to their designation; (*b*) and are conferred *not with the intention* of producing the true, that is to say, sacrificial [1] priesthood of the New Testament. This decision, it maintains, was already pronounced in the sixteenth century on the ground of an examination of the Anglican Ordinal. This examination has been repeated at the present time, and on the ground of it the Pope repeats the negative judgement of the Roman Catholic Church upon this matter. The whole of the Anglican *Responsio* centres in the following propositions. In the Church of Christ *there has never been a definite form* for conferring the priesthood, and the Roman Church herself has not always used one and the same *form*, while on the other hand she herself at the present time acknowledges the Orders of the Eastern Christians (Greeks, Russians, Maronites, Copts, Armenians, &c.) as valid, although the *forms* of their ordinations differ. The difference of *form* comes from the fact that in ancient times national Churches enjoyed liberty to draw up the *forms* for accomplishing the Sacraments (with the exception of the Sacrament of Baptism); and this right national Churches cannot be deprived of. The present forms of the Anglican Ordinal correspond entirely to their designations: in them the degree in the hierarchy to which the ordinand is to be raised is definitely indicated, and his future rights and powers are clearly defined. The changes introduced into the Ordinal do not affect the essence of the sacred act. Moreover, the historical conclusions of the Pope are insufficiently well founded, inasmuch as there are no undoubted historical data to base them upon.

---

[1] This term (жертвоприношение) is not used by the Pope; it is used in the *Vindication* and in the introductory letter [to the Russian Bishops] of Cardinal Vaughan. It is a translation of the word " sacrificial."

The authors of the *Vindication*, as Cardinal Vaughan says in his letter addressed to the representatives of the Orthodox Church, *" desired to draw the attention of the Anglican Archbishops to certain points on which they had seriously misunderstood the arguments used by the Pope."* They also desired *to indicate more fully the main grounds of the Papal decision* out of the mass of evidence collected by a Roman Catholic commission at the time that the question of Anglican Orders was being investigated; and, lastly, *to bring the controversy to a direct issue* by pointing out a question to which a clear and definite answer must be given.

In spite, however, of the limits which they lay down for their *Vindication*, its authors begin it by a disquisition upon a question which was not touched upon in the *Responsio* of the Anglicans to the Papal Bull, namely, the question of a supreme authority in the Church of Christ, indispensable for the final settlement of questions concerning matters of faith; the authors of the *Vindication* argue that no one else but the Pope has any such authority, and that no one else can take upon himself the settlement of a question concerning the Sacraments, including the Sacrament of Orders. In view of the invitation by the authors of the *Vindication* to judge of the force of their arguments upon their own merit, it behoves us to say that the decrees of the Pope have no obligatory force for the whole Church so long as the authority of a General Council does not recognize them as having such force. But by this very authority [i. e. a General Council] the region subject to the jurisdiction of the Bishop of Rome has been repeatedly defined [1]. Of course we do not deny the right of the Bishop of Rome to pronounce his judgement in matters which concern the local Churches placed under his jurisdiction; such a right belongs to every Bishop of the Church of God, who is enjoined by the Holy Ghost to " preach the Word, to be instant in season and out of season, to reprove, rebuke and exhort, with all longsuffering " (2 Tim. iv. 2). But not one of them can set forth a decision obligatory for the whole Church of Christ, just as it is not Peter, nor Paul, nor James, nor John, but a council of them which, with the good pleasure of the Holy Ghost, decrees that the people of Antioch are not to have a superfluous burden laid upon them (Acts xv. 23–28). We highly appreciate the sincere desire of all for reunion with the true flock

[1] Conc. Nic. I, Can. 6; Conc. Constant. I, Can. 2 and 3; Conc. Chalc., Can. 28. The Thirty-fourth Apostolic Canon also applies here.

of Christ under the rule of the one Shepherd and Chief-Shepherd (John x. 16, 1 Peter v. 4), and especially of those who are striving to remove hindrances to the reunion of all Christians in one Church; and therefore we highly appreciate the pains taken by the Roman Catholic Bishops to bring about a clearer and more accurate understanding of the origin and essence of the present Anglican hierarchy; and with all our souls we rejoice that, thanks to the latest investigations, both on the Roman Catholic and the Anglican sides, the necessity has been got rid of of deciding the question of lawfulness and reality of the successional laying on of hands which took place upon Parker, from whom the present Anglican hierarchy traces its descent. The Pope in his Bull passes by the history of Parker's consecration in complete silence; the vindicators of the Bull confine themselves to a short remark upon it; they, however, somewhat weaken the significance of the Pope's silence by mentioning that even without these grounds the invalidity of Anglican Orders was decisively proved. In view of this attitude towards the question of Parker's consecration [1] in the official documents, the science of ecclesiastical history may at the present time put this question finally aside from its discussions, and occupy itself only with the second, that is to say, the dogmatic side of the question of the validity of Anglican Orders.

Into the controversy about Anglican Orders they quite unexpectedly introduce the question of the attitude of the Papal authority to Anglican Ordinations in the sixteenth century. Pope Leo XIII in his Bull brought forward some data by way of historical reference. The Anglican Archbishops in their *Answer* to the Bull treated this question as being of minor importance in comparison to the question of the essence of the Anglican Ordinal [2]. As they in general rejected the position that the practice of the Roman Church had any bearing upon the solution of the question, they might very well have left the historical investigations of the Pope on one side; however, they, on the contrary, devote a considerable space to them, and investigate them extremely carefully; and this, in the first place, because in the teaching of the Pope Eugenius IV concerning the Sacrament of Orders there

---

[1] Amongst the Bishops that consecrated Parker there was one who had been consecrated according to the Roman Catholic rite; see Denny and Lacey, *De hierarchia Anglicana,* pp. 11–14; Sokoloff, *Hierarchy,* pp. 81, 84, 88–90.

[2] *Answer,* § v.

is an important disagreement with the teaching of Pope Leo XIII, and secondly, because the historical conclusions of Leo XIII appeared to them to be insufficiently grounded upon facts. The authors of the *Vindication* say that they do not wish to extend the limits of the question, both because the data already mentioned are quite sufficient for its solution, and also because a detailed investigation of this question would necessarily lead to the investigation of technical details not easy for the mass of readers to follow [1]. They leave open the question of the missing documents, which was raised by the Anglican Archbishops in their *Answer* [2]; all they do is to analyze in greater detail the documents mentioned by the Pope, draw the same conclusion from them, and in proof of the correctness of this conclusion bring forward the testimony of two writers of the sixteenth century, the Roman Catholic Bonner [3] and the Protestant Pilkington. The testimony of the latter is especially important, in view of the fact that the Anglicans likewise quote him in support of their views [4]. It seems to us that the explanation of the Anglican Archbishops is the more natural, and states the meaning of the passage quoted from this writer more accurately than does the explanation of the Roman Catholics. In reply to the statement that under Cardinal Pole a very small number of persons were reordained, the authors of the *Vindication* say that in the registers of the archives of the time of Queen Mary the names of thirteen or fourteen clergymen are inscribed who received a fresh ordination in the dioceses of London and Oxford alone. The enumeration of persons who were degraded in the reign of Queen Mary on account, as it were, of the *nullity* of their Orders, adds considerable weight to this part of their argument. But the argument itself is, to a considerable degree, weakened by contrary facts [5], which testify in general to the indefinite and inconsistent character of the attitude of the Roman Catholics towards the Anglican hierarchy during the period of the Roman Catholic reaction; and this inconsistency of practice resulted from the inconsistency of the guiding rules of the Roman

---

[1] *Vindication*, § 7 (p. 11).   [2] *Answer*, § vi.

[3] One of the most zealous defenders of Roman Catholicism and fiercest opponents of the Reformation in the sixteenth century.

[4] *Answer*, § vi. note 1.

[5] See *De hierarchia Anglicana*, pp. 160-168; compare Sokoloff, *op. cit.*, pp. 117-119 [and W. H. Frere, *The Marian Reaction*, passim. W. E. C.]

Church; for Cardinal Pole, it can hardly be doubted, was also guided by the decree of Pope Eugenius IV concerning the Armenians; in which case he would have to reordain even those who had been ordained by the ancient Roman Pontifical[1]. In any case, the conclusion drawn from the whole matter is to the effect that the chief hindrance to acknowledging the validity of Anglican Ordinations was already, in the sixteenth century, considered to lie in peculiarities of the Order of Service with which they were performed. And the authors of the Bull consider the same thing to have been the case in the matter of Gordon at the beginning of the eighteenth century. This matter, before it was put before Clement XI to decide, was subjected to a careful examination in the Congregation of Sacred Rites. Pope Clement XI decreed that Gordon (who had been an Anglican Bishop) *must be ordained anew and unconditionally in all degrees (of the hierarchy), beginning with the lowest.* This is how Pope Leo XIII represents the matter in his Bull. The Anglican Archbishops say that this affair, which is in itself obscure, is rendered still more so by the personality of Gordon, who was seeking to obtain a post which would bring him in money from the Roman Church. In his petition he committed a crime, inasmuch as he calumniated the Anglican Ordinal, while the Congregation of Sacred Rites gave its decision upon this matter without having made due inquiries, and at the same time contradicting its own regulation[2] on the matter of Abyssinian Orders. The Vindicators of the Bull declare that the affair of Gordon was settled on the ground of an investigation of the Anglican Ordinal in 1685 by Cardinal Casanata. His *votum* and *relatio* constituted the actual documents upon which the Gordon affair was settled. But upon the question of the Abyssinians and Armenians the *Vindication* speaks in another place, as we shall presently see.

Having adjusted the matter of the documentary and historical deficiencies of Leo XIII's Bull, the authors of the *Vindication* pass on to the principal part of its contents—to the question of the defects to be discovered in the Anglican Ordinal. To this question the principal part of the Bull is devoted; and to it likewise is given the most important place in the Anglican *Answer;* and so in the

---

[1] Sokoloff, *op. cit.,* pp. 119-123, gives another explanation of this state of affairs.

[2] [въ своемъ постановлении рѣшения, *literally,* regulation of the solution. W. J. B.]

Vindication it is given the chief place. In our opinion this question does not in the least deserve the amount of attention that the Bull of Leo XIII devotes to it, if one is to put the matter in the same way as the Pope has done. Recognizing the necessary appurtenances of each sacrament to be its *matter* (material, or material sign), its *form* (the words used on the employment of the matter), and lastly, the *intention* to perform the Sacrament in the sense in which the Church intends it, Pope Leo XIII was obliged to acknowledge that the *matter* is something indefinite, and which may take various *forms*, or may be united with various *forms*; and therefore it has not such an essential significance in defining the validity of the Sacrament of Orders as has the *form*. But, as the *Answer* of the Anglican Archbishops points out, in the Church of Christ—so far as the records of its past life are known to us—there both have been and still are various *forms* of ordination, and in this respect the Roman Church herself cannot be said to be a pattern of continuity or consistency, because her present *form* of ordination has only existed from the sixteenth century (that is, from the time of the Council of Trent); and it was composed at various periods. Pope Eugenius IV (fifteenth century), for instance, instructs the Armenians, that the *matter* of the Sacrament is the porrection of the instruments, and that the *form* is: "Receive authority to accomplish sacrifice in the Church for the living and the dead." Lastly, the Roman Church has recognized and still recognizes as valid the ordinations of the various Eastern Christians, whose *forms* of ordination do not correspond to the requirements laid down in the Pope's Bull. All this is true ; and from the formal point of view the *Answer* of the Anglican Archbishops is irresistible. And therefore the authors of the *Vindication* were obliged to alter the way of putting the question. We have already seen that in their doctrine of the essentially necessary properties of the Order of laying on of hands they introduce a doctrine of the nature of the hierarchy of the New Covenant, and of the nature of the Sacrament of the Eucharist, and draw up their *Vindication* of the Bull pretty nearly in the following form : Inasmuch as the Anglican doctrine of the Eucharist excludes the idea of it being the sacrifice of the New Covenant, in this doctrine there cannot be room for the doctrine of a true priesthood. The question being put in this way, it will now be found possible without difficulty to find a satisfactory reply in defence of the Bull against Anglican attacks. Moreover, in this way of putting the question, the authors of the *Vindication* see nothing new, but merely a development of the ideas expressed in the Pope's Bull, and they reproach the Anglican Archbishops with not having understood this. This is to a certain degree true, for the Pope attacks the Anglicans very vigorously for excluding from their Ordinal and their Form for administering the Sacrament of the Eucharist, just those passages where mention is made of the priesthood being appointed for the purpose of offering the sacrifice of the New Covenant. In our opinion the following way of putting the question is the only right and expedient one. As a matter of fact, if the Anglican Order of Ordination of a priest and of a bishop presents a whole list of references concerning the priesthood and the office of a bishop, then why argue that these ideas are excluded from it? Even the Ordinal of 1550, for which the Pope levels his chief attacks upon the Anglican Reformers, is, as it seems to us, entirely irreproachable in this respect. Here are the proofs of it. At the time of the ordination of presbyters Acts xx. 17–35 is read, which speaks of the conversation of the holy Apostle Paul *with the* Ephesian *presbyters* at Miletus, or from 1 Tim. iii, which speaks of the qualities of *a bishop*; the Gospel from Matt. xxviii. 18–20 is read : "*All power is given Me in heaven and in earth. Go ye therefore,*" &c., or from John x : "*Verily, verily, I say unto you, he that entereth not by the door into the sheepfold,*" . . . or John xx : "*The same day at evening*" . . . After this the hymn, *Veni Creator Spiritus,* is sung. After the presentation of the candidate for ordination, the Bishop says to the people : *Good people, these be they whom we purpose, God willing, to receive this day unto the holy Office of Priesthood;* and in the prayer which follows : *Mercifully behold these Thy servants now called to the Office of Priesthood.* . . . After the promise follows a number of questions, amongst which one *of ministering the Sacraments as the Lord hath commanded*[1]; further on, there follows a prayer for strength

[1] We are examining the Order for the ordaining of a priest and of a bishop, because these are the Orders with which we are principally concerned. The following is one of the questions put to a candidate for Deacon's Orders : *It pertaineth to the office of a Deacon . . . to assist the Priest in Divine Service, and specially when he ministereth the holy Communion . . . to read holy Scriptures and Homilies, . . . to instruct the youth in the Catechism, . . . to baptize and to preach if he be admitted thereto by the Bishop. . . . Will you do this gladly and willingly?* Whereas the corresponding question

and power for those who are now to be ordained to perform the same, and afterwards the actual laying on of hands with the words: *Receive the Holy Ghost; whose sins thou dost forgive, they are forgiven; and whose sins thou dost retain, they are retained. And be thou a faithful Dispenser of the Word of God, and of His holy Sacraments; in the Name of the Father, and of the Son, and of the Holy Ghost. Amen.* While these words are being pronounced, the candidate for Priest's Orders is kneeling, and the Bishop with the presbyters who are serving with him hold their hands on his head. After this the Bishop delivers a Bible to the newly ordained priest, saying: *Take thou authority to preach the Word of God, and to minister the holy Sacraments. . . .* In the Order for the Consecration of a Bishop, the idea that *the Episcopate is the continuation of the ministry of the Apostles* is drawn out. Thus the readings from Scripture are taken from 1 Tim. iii. and John xxi. 15: "*Jesus said to Simon Peter: Simon, son of Jonas, lovest thou Me?*" . . . After the presentation of the Bishop elect by two Bishops, the Archbishop who is to consecrate him pronounces a short address in which he speaks of the choosing of the Apostles by Jesus Christ, and of the laying on of hands upon Barnabas and Paul; after the Litany a prayer is read, in which the newly elected is spoken of as "*called to the work and ministry of a Bishop.*" The actual consecration takes place by means of the laying on of the hands of all the Bishops present upon the head of the candidate, while the Archbishop pronounces the words: *Take the Holy Ghost, and remember that thou stir up the grace of God which is in thee by imposition of hands: for God hath not given us the spirit of fear, but of power, and love, and of soberness* (2 Tim. i. 6, 7). After this follows the delivery of a Bible to the newly consecrated Bishop with words which speak of the necessity of a careful study of the sacred Books, and meditation upon them, &c. In the final prayer (after the Communion) a heavenly blessing upon the newly consecrated Bishop is once more prayed for, and the sending down upon him of the grace of the Holy Spirit [1]. . . . From these extracts alone, taken from

asked of the candidate for Priest's Orders is: *Will you then give your faithful diligence always so to minister . . . the Sacraments . . . of Christ, as the Lord hath commanded . . . according to the Commandments of God?*

[1] The extracts have been taken from *The Book of Common Prayer, A.D. 1886*, compared with the first Prayer Book of King Edward VI, A.D. 1549*, ed. with introduction by W. Miles Mirze, Lond. 1887, pp. 325-356 (the first columns of

the first, in point of time, of the Anglican Orders, one can see sufficiently well that its compilers (*a*) distinguished the ministry of a priest and of a deacon from the ministry of a bishop; (*b*) that to the ministry of a priest they gave the name "*the Holy Office of the Priesthood*," agreeably with the most ancient use of this word; (*c*) that to the duties of the ministry of a priest, amongst others, they referred the administration of the Holy Sacraments of God, and the preaching of the Word of God; (*d*) that they compared the Episcopate to the Apostolate, and consequently saw in the latter the source of the hierarchy in succession from them; (*e*) that they regarded God the Father Almighty through the Holy Ghost as the First Source of the hierarchy. What they understood by these terms is quite another matter.

It is just this question *as to what the Anglicans understand by these terms* which must be the only question, which must of necessity be solved, in order either to admit or to reject the possibility of the reunion of the Anglicans with those Christian communities which regard the hierarchy as the priesthood of the New Covenant. In respect to the unbroken handing on of grace (through the Roman Church from the Apostles) in Anglican Ordinations there cannot now even be a doubt, when once the Anglican hierarchy is admitted to draw its origin from persons who really had received the grace of the hierarchy, which, according to Roman Catholic teaching, is indelible [1]. The Bishops that consecrated Parker, one of whom was consecrated according to the rite of the Roman Catholic Church, were themselves consecrated with the object (*intention*) of the handing on to them of the grace of the hierarchy, and they consecrated Parker with *the intention* of communicating to him this gift of grace. Accordingly Parker also had the grace of the hierarchy in unbroken succession, and those who received ordination from him must, from the Roman Catholic point of view, be acknowledged to possess this grace. From this it follows that the practice of the

the year 1549), and from Appendix V to the book *De hierarchia Anglicana* by Denny and Lacey, Londini 1895, pp. 226-244.

[1] The Roman Catholic theologians set forth as the ground of this doctrine the definition of the Council of Trent (sess. 23, cap. 3) and from it arrive, as a logical deduction, at their conclusion concerning the indelible character of the grace of the Episcopate (*potestas indelebilis*), vide Tepe, S. J., *Institutiones Theologicae*, vol. iv. pp. 572-6; Paris 1898; Knol a Bulsano, *Institutiones Theologiae Theoreticae*, vol. ii. pp. 323-7, col. 2, Aug. Taurin. 1890.

Roman Church in respect to the Anglicans contradicts their own
doctrine concerning the indelibility of the grace of the priesthood
(*character indelebilis, initerabilis*, &c.), and concerning the validity
of a sacrament[1] administered by a heretic or even a heathen ("an
unbaptized man," as it is put in Leo XIII's Bull), provided that he
has a sincere intention of accomplishing that which the Church wishes
to accomplish. We therefore think that all the investigations of the
Roman Catholics upon the question of Anglican Orders ought to have
been concentrated upon the question as to the unbrokenness of
the actual succession in the matter of the laying on of hands, and
when once its uninterruptedness had been established, the Anglican
hierarchy ought to have been recognized by the Roman Catholics
as having a valid significance. But for the solution of the question
of the reunion of Anglicanism with one of those Churches which
have an uninterrupted hierarchical succession from the Apostles,
it is indispensable to solve the question as to what degree of
heresy the doctrine of the Anglicans has reached, and in particular
their doctrine concerning the Sacraments, in which of course
is included their teaching concerning the Sacrament of Orders.
As in the Papal Bull, so also especially in the *Vindication*, these
questions are still mixed up, although the possibility of separating
them is indicated. The *Vindication* of the Papal Bull, as compared with the Bull itself, makes a significant step forward, inasmuch as it leaves the historico-canonical side of the question
almost entirely on one side, and that its principal part consists of
dogmatic questions in respect to the Sacrament of the Eucharist
and the New Testament priesthood. The way in which these
questions are solved is by a comparison of the doctrine of the
Anglicans with the doctrine of the Roman Catholics. As a result
of this comparison a profound difference is pointed out, while
as a final deduction in application to the doctrine concerning
Anglican Orders their invalidity is declared. But if we turn our
attention to the fact that all the symbolical books of the Roman
Catholics, and in accordance with them the Roman Catholic theologians, speak of the special character of grace in the Sacrament
of Orders—that is to say, if we hold in view the fact that, according to the teaching of the Roman Catholics, Orders constitute

---

[1] [The original has свящеиства, *priesthood*: but this is evidently a misprint
for тaииства, *a sacrament*. W. J. B.]

a special and completely independent "most noble" (*nobilissimum*) Sacrament, which communicates a special kind of grace [1], independent of the gifts of grace bestowed in the other Sacraments, and even conditioning the presence of grace in the other Sacraments, (for he who has not himself received the gift of grace in the Sacrament of Orders can neither communicate that gift to others nor accomplish the other Sacraments [2])—in this case it is necessary to arrive at an entirely inverse conclusion ; namely, that the validity of Orders does not depend upon the validity of the Sacrament of the Eucharist, but, on the contrary, that upon the validity of the grace living in the minister, and given him by means of the laying on of the hands of the presbytery (1 Tim. iv. 14), depends the possibility of affording valid, and not merely sham, Sacraments. The authors of the *Vindication* leave this fact entirely out of sight, and the reproach contained in the Anglican Archbishops' reply is a perfectly just one. To tell the truth, the *Vindication* of the Bull is not a vindication in the proper sense of the word ; it is a fresh objection brought against Anglicanism by the Roman Catholics, not, however, from the point of view of historico-canonical data, on the ground of which it might be possible to arrive at the recognition of Anglican Orders, but from the point of view of dogmatic principles, which would give them the right to contemplate Anglicanism as a Protestant sect. For this reason we admit its very great importance, as being one of those official documents from the Roman Catholic side which, together with Leo XIII's Bull, put an end, in a sense favourable for the Anglicans, to the historico-canonical side of the question of the validity of Anglican Orders; but at the same time the *Vindication* subjects their validity in their essence to serious doubt, in view of Anglican doctrine concerning the Sacraments. The authors of the *Vindication* at the end of it put a question to the Anglicans ; what this question is we already know. We wish also to say that it is an entirely superfluous question. The Thirty-Nine Articles teach very clearly about the Sacraments,

---

[1] *Concil. Trid.* sess. 23, *sacram. ord.* can. 3, 4, 7.—*Catechismus Romanus,* pars 2, cap. viii; quest. ii, xviii, xxxiv (and in general the whole section : *de Ordinis sacramento*). Bellarminus in the doctrine of the Sacrament of Orders, cap. 5, and the treatises on the Sacrament of Orders in the works of Tepe and Knol a Balsano from which we have already quoted.

[2] See *Orthodox Confession,* I, questions 100, 109, 118. Epistle of the Eastern Patriarchs, Arts. x, xvii, and the Roman Catholic treatises already mentioned.

and teach inconsistently both with the Orthodox Church and with Roman Catholicism, while the practice of the Anglicans, as shown in the solution of matters concerning the so-called Ritualists, speaks for the fact that this doctrine is binding upon all Anglicans[1]. From hence the direct and only conclusion to be drawn is that for the reunion of the Anglicans with the Orthodox Church it is necessary that they for their part should acknowledge the true doctrine with regard to all that the ancient universal Church believed, and consequently that they must reject the doctrine of the *Filioque* and correct their teaching with regard to the sources of Christian doctrine, with regard to faith and good works, and with regard to the Sacraments. The rest of their errors will then disappear of their own accord. This amending is already taking place, slowly, it is true, but still uninterruptedly ; it is going on in the movement known under the name of .... *holiness*, often incorrectly styled *Ritualism*. It is indispe.... ' .... the Archbishops of England should not only not hinder this movement, but, on the contrary, that they should in every way co-operate with it, because there is the hope that with its aid Anglicanism may purge itself not only of its Protestant errors, but also from those many mediaeval novelties which have separated the English people from their mother the primitive Catholic Church of the first nine centuries of her history.

In conclusion, we will say a few words about the explanations of historical documents in the *Vindication*. We have already mentioned that, appended to it, there is an explanation of certain passages of the letter of Pope Julius III to Cardinal Pole. In this letter no definite directions are given with regard to Anglican Ordinations, and conclusions favourable to Roman Catholic practice can only be arrived at by the aid of theoretical considerations ; but the complete silence of other documents upon this subject give one the right to conclude that Cardinal Pole *did not re-ordain* all unconditionally, and that definitely expressed full powers to do so were not given him : full powers were given him to act according to his personal judgement, using the authority of the Apostolic See for the purpose. And, therefore, the authors of the *Vindication* have left the objection of the Anglicans, expressed

---

[1] See our article in *Transactions of Kieff Eccl. Acad.*, 1897, " New Religious Transformations in England " (July-Sept.).

in the words, "Where, for example, are the faculties granted to Pole after August 5, 1553, and before March 8, 1554 [1]," unanswered as far as the essence of the question is concerned. They found themselves in a still greater difficulty, in view of the fact that Pope Leo XIII reckons the matter of the Sacrament of Orders to be the laying on of hands, while Pope Eugenius IV reckons it to be the porrection of the instruments; Pope Eugenius IV reckons as the *form* the words: "Receive authority to offer sacrifices in the Church for the quick and dead"; Pope Leo XIII is altogether silent about the *form*, inasmuch as upon this subject there is no definite teaching in the Roman Catholic Church. The Roman Catechism inclines towards the recognition of Pope Eugenius' definition; while meanwhile, it is *in the form* that, according to the words of Leo XIII, a definition of the essential nature of the Sacrament must be sought [2]. The explanation of the disagreements of Papal definitions upon this subject given by the authors of the *Vindication* is wide enough, and amounts to this: that Pope Eugenius acknowledged the laying on of hands also to be the matter of the Sacrament, and only mentioned the porrection of the instruments because with the Armenians, with whom this definition was concerned, the porrection of instruments does not come in their rite of Ordination, whereas the laying on of hands does. This explanation is too far-fetched, and invites a number of perplexed questions, which had been asked by the Anglicans even before the publication of the Papal Bull [3]. The authors of the *Vindication* ought to have solved these questions, if their arguments upon this point were to be acknowledged as convincing. The resolution on the affair of the Abyssinian Ordinations, which was decreed by Clement XI in 1704, is altogether contradictory to the resolution of the same Pope in the affair of Gordon, the Anglican Bishop, inasmuch as the Pope in the first resolution admits the validity of Ordinations administered by the laying on of hands, combined only with the words, "Receive the Holy Ghost," and with a prayer in which no use is made of the words *presbyterate* or *priesthood*, but only in words corresponding to the idea of *leaders* [4] (translated by the word *seniores*). The *Vindication*

---

[1] [*Answer*, § vi. W. E. C.]

[2] See the Bull *Apostolicae Curae*, § 7.

[3] *De hierarchia Anglicana*, by Denny and Lacey, pp. 111–114.

[4] ["that he may direct Thy people even as Thou didst bid Moses to choose

maintains that such *a form* the Roman See never sanctioned, and with sufficient reason surmises that the words indicating the priesthood in the Order of Abyssinian Ordinations of priests may have been dropped out in the translation[1]. But for a final solution of this misunderstanding, either no data exist, or else they have not been allowed to see the light by the Sacred Congregation of Rites. The whole explanation given by the authors of the *Vindication* of this affair is in reality nothing but a series of conjectures, which hardly at all get rid of the objections raised by the Anglicans[2]. In the fourth Appendix there are collected some extracts from various ancient forms of Ordination. They are brought forward by the *Vindication* for the purpose of demonstrating the insufficiency of the Anglican *form* by means of comparison. It seems to us, that the comparing of these prayers together leads rather to a conclusion favourable to the Anglicans, because only in the Nestorian, Armenian, and ancient Gallican *forms* of Ordination is mention made of the offering of sacrifice as the duty of the priest, and moreover only the Armenian prayer speaks of "consecrating the awful and holy Sacrament of the Body and Blood of our Lord and Saviour Jesus Christ"; while the ancient Gallican prayer speaks of "transforming the bread and wine into the Body and Blood of Thy Son[3]." Moreover, the authors of the *Vindication* say[4], that this last form is only conjectural, and that for the Consecration of Bishops, according to this Order, no prayers whatever have been preserved. The last Appendix is concerned with the seventeenth Article of the "Letter of the Eastern Patriarchs concerning the orthodox Faith." This Article is quoted by the authors of the *Vindication* according to Dr. Neale's translation, from the Russian text into English, with indication of the variations from it contained in a German translation made by the Archpriest Maltzeff, and in the Greek original of the "Letter." The authors of the *Vindication*

---

leaders for Thy chosen people." See the Abyssinian Form for the Priesthood in *Vindication*, p. 96. W. E. C.]

[1] See *Vindication*, p. 96, footnote.

[2] Compare *Vindication*, pp. 89-92, with *De hierarchia Anglicana*, by Denny and Lacey, pp. 245-249.

[3] [For the gradual modifications of this prayer see *Priesthood in the English Church*, p. 47, and the Table at p. 56. W. E. C.]

[4] [*Vindication*, p. 97. W. E. C.]

are at special pains to set forth the idea[1] that the teaching of the Orthodox Church concerning transubstantiation[2] ($\mu\epsilon\tau o\upsilon\sigma\iota\omega\sigma\iota s$) and a propitiatory sacrifice is that which is rejected by Anglican divines from the sixteenth century downwards and by the Articles on the Eucharist (i. e. 28, 29, 30, 31), but which is recognized by Roman Catholicism.

[1] [Literally, "with special force tint this idea, that," &c. W. J. B.]
[2] [пресуществленiе. W. J. B.]

IV.

Accordingly, the question of Anglican hierarchy at the present time is in the following position:—

(1) Its uninterrupted succession from and connexion with the Roman Catholic hierarchy, thanks to the latest historical investigations, must be acknowledged to be undoubted.

(2) It is quite true that this connexion is as yet not acknowledged by the Roman Catholics, but already it is not openly rejected in documents which are generally binding upon Roman Catholics [1], such, for instance, as the Bull *Apostolicae Curae.*

(3) The Anglican Ordinal, in respect to its contents, may be placed amongst that series of forms of Ordination which are used by those Christian bodies whose hierarchy, notwithstanding their heresy, is admitted by the Roman Catholics to be valid.

(4) For the reunion of the Anglicans with those Christian bodies which have a hierarchy of unbroken Apostolical succession, before all things, the restoration by the Anglicans of the true faith—that is to say the teaching of the ancient universal Church—is necessary. If *the Church of Christ is a community, instituted by our Lord Jesus Christ, of men believing on Him, united amongst themselves by the unity of the faith, the unity of the hierarchy, and the unity of the Sacraments* [2], then, in order that the Anglicans may be reunited with the true Church of Christ, it is indispensable that they

---

[1] [Literally, "documents having for Roman Catholics a general-obligatory significance." W. J. B.]

[2] Compare the definition of the Church in the *Epistle of the Eastern Patriarchs*, art. x; Bishop Antonius, *Dogmatic Theology*, § 249; Bishop Macarius, *Introduction to Orthodox Theology*, §§ 16-20, and § 134; Bishop Plato, *Shortened Exposition of Dogmatic Faith*, Kostroma 1869, p. 103; Philaret, Archbishop of Chernigoff, *Orthodox Dogmatic Theology*, § 290 (p. 355); and the *Orthodox Christian Catechism* on the question "What is the Church?"

should restore their union with her in the faith and in the Sacraments. And if the teaching of the present Anglican Episcopate upon the Sacrament of Orders turns out to agree with the teaching of the ancient universal Church, this will be a clear proof that Anglicanism has not merely preserved the Apostolical succession in an outward manner, but that it has not changed the essential nature of that ministry which is indispensable for the Church according to the mind of her Divine Founder and Head. Only then will it be possible to decide the question as to what order of error the errors of the Anglican Church are to be referred; this is to say, whether the gift of the grace of the priesthood has been extinguished within her, or whether this Church still has within her a glimmering of the light of grace, sufficient to enable her Orders to be acknowledged as valid [1].

And so, in order to arrive at a final settlement of the question of the Anglican hierarchy, it is indispensable that the question should be settled of the beliefs of this hierarchy upon the Sacraments instituted by the Lord, to the number of which is to be referred the Sacrament of Orders itself, which serves as the means of grace for the planting of the priesthood in the Church. We

---

[1] The question of the extinction of grace in communities which have separated themselves from the Church would, it would seem, have to be decided against Anglicanism, in view of the clear reply of St. Basil the Great to Amphilochius, which applies to all non-Orthodox confessions. This holy Doctor and Father of the Universal Church says: "Although the beginning of separation from the Church was in consequence of a schism, yet those who had left the Church already no longer possessed the Spirit of grace, inasmuch as its transmission has been impoverished on account of the interruption of the succession : and although those who first separated themselves had received the Orders from the Fathers, and through the imposition of their hands had received a spiritual gift, yet having taken themselves away, and having made themselves laymen, they no longer had the power either to christen or to ordain, and were not in a condition to hand on to others that grace of the Holy Spirit from which they themselves had fallen away" [S. Basil. *Epist.* clxxxviii. *ad Amphil.* § 1. The Russian version quoted by Prof. Bulgakoff is not very accurate, since the original runs : διότι ἡ μὲν ἀρχὴ τοῦ χωρισμοῦ διὰ σχίσματος γέγονεν· οἱ δὲ τῆς Ἐκκλησίας ἀποστάντες κ.τ.λ. W. E. C.] It is true that the ancient Universal Church sometimes softened down this severe judgement upon heretics with a view to attracting them (e. g. the Nestorians) to herself; but this was done only according to the decrees of the Church, and not according to the desires of private persons. Consequently, in the present case, the final decision of the question rests with the Church, and not with her individual representatives.

have hopes, that love for truth, love for unity and peace in the Church, will without delay rouse the representatives of the Anglican hierarchy to afford their support to all who are searching for the truth in the explanation of questions concerning the doctrinal teaching of the Anglicans—questions, which even to the present time remain unsolved.

A. BULGAKOFF.

OXFORD : HORACE HART

PRINTER TO THE UNIVERSITY

www.ingramcontent.com/pod-product-compliance
Lightning Source LLC
Chambersburg PA
CBHW021428090426
42739CB00009B/1391